But God,
I Don't Love Me !

Key To Fulfilling
Jesus' Great Commandment

PAUL F. ALLEN

WESTBOW
P R E S S
A DIVISION OF THOMAS NELSON

WestBow Press books may be ordered through booksellers or by contacting:

WestBow Press
A Division of Thomas Nelson
1663 Liberty Drive
Bloomington, IN 47403
www.westbowpress.com
1-(866) 928-1240

ISBN: 978-1-4497-9217-6 (sc)
ISBN: 978-1-4497-9218-3 (e)

Library of Congress Control Number: 2013907104

Printed in the United States of America.

WestBow Press rev. date: 05/02/2013

Table of Contents

Introduction

Most of us are familiar with Jesus' admonition to a lawyer about God's priority in life. Though being the great commandment, it demonstrates God's plan and desire for our true place in His kingdom and creation. "You must love the Lord your God with all your heart, with all your soul and all your mind. This is the first and greatest commandment. A second is equally important: Love your neighbor as yourself." (Matt. 22:37–39) On the surface it seems too great an obstacle for many of us to love our neighbor as we love ourselves. This is designed to put us in a receiving relationship with our Creator God.

How often have each of us heard it said that we cannot give away that which we do not have? With probably no disputation to this truth, when one is wounded with a disturbing challenge, it does seem just a little bit cold and legalistic. It tends to rule out divine grace in a willing life. Our mental institutions are filled with people who have no clue about accepting or recognizing their own worth. Psychiatrists are doing a land office business. These patients often were brainwashed into self-condemnation and experienced a critical shortage of any praise. Many made a mistake, often a damaging act, and have no mental, emotional, or spiritual resources to deal with it, compounded by perpetual criticism from others.

If one is to grasp any semblance of what it means to truly love someone else, many things have to take place. The pitiful truth is how so many will willingly carry around all sorts of excess baggage, making them basically ineffective in social interaction. They often learn somehow to cope with this burden, and begin to believe it is their lot in life. One may legitimately ask if they believe that dragging the baggage is acceptable to our Creator God. Without a doubt this is a challenge to see how personal God is to us. Are we really candidates for a de-programming, or would washing and healing be our answer? Shouldn't we discover God as the One who is, in the Greek, our 'sodzo', or deliverer? What would it do for us to learn from the Hebrew language that He is Jehovah Shalam, the Lord our Restorer?

Indeed, "wherever the Spirit of the Lord is, he gives freedom."

(II Corinthians 3:17) Our greatest desire is that this writing be the encouragement that you need to set you free, free to love and forgive yourself and others.

They Always Say That

It always seems that there is no shortage of people who are willing to speak their minds regardless of where or how it lands. At our objective best we can even recall few instances where good people, even born-again Christians, felt they were trying to be helpful with their advice or *counsel*. What transpires is that the end result was counter-productive to the well-being of the recipient. Why is it that people are always so quick to say, "Just be strong", or "You just gotta pray more"? That will probably fall on deaf ears, or be dismissed as mere religious jargon.

One of the more familiar phrases which seem very prevalent in the Body of Christ is, "Johnny, don't you know you have to love yourself before you can really love others?". Here we are quickly faced with "Love your neighbor as yourself." There may well be truth in this statement, but somehow it appears to be more well-equipped with a good set of brakes. One can easily become defensive and think, "For crying out loud, you mean what good I've tried to do up to now is all for naught?". Quite often, particularly among Christians, this advice is aimed at people who may well be Christians, but have struggled in their walk and attempts to help others because of internal road blocks. These hindrances often go unnoticed or misunderstood. The strugglers don't need, at this point, condemnation or legalism. Challenges like the previous quotation can easily be boiled down to the blind leading the blind. Among church circles it is easy to make sanctimonious remarks because they sound biblical or saintly. It should be remembered that Jesus declared that our mouths reveal what our hearts are full of. (Matt. 12:34)

Hoping For Hope

G od's choice and plan is for any and all to be in unity with Him and each other in Christ Jesus. Again the struggling Christian must discover, proclaim and hang on to the scripture which reassures us that "So now there is no condemnation for those who belong to Christ Jesus". (Rom. 8:1) This is and should be good news to any who receive it. The issue seems to be that all born-again persons are members of the Body of Christ, who is the Head. When a member is hurting or possibly inoperative, the other members are to respond with mercy and help. What the troubled don't need is the insensitive response, "You just gotta have more faith". The design of the unifying Savior must follow through with its blueprint of being redemptive and mutually supportive. Of a truth, this ministry is often a pattern demonstrated by a compassionate shepherd, the pastor, consistently and persistently.

As a fellow church member, let us suppose that we have discerned accurately that Johnny Doe is a good and accepted member of the Body. However, it has become evident that he has a low opinion of himself and lacks effectiveness and victory. Should we throw platitudes at him, hoping that he will wake up to something beneficial? There is probably a damaging history behind his wounded self image. Our enemy, satan the opportunist, has taken advantage of this. Though they may not readily recognize it, people who are wounded and negative have an inner yearning for a healing and restoration. This is the pursuit of the soul and spirit.

Probably the most liberating aspect in a plethora of 'good advice' and religious platitudes is coming to the place of discovering what is really real. We shall toss out the physiological meanderings of those who proudly assert, "One creates his own reality". If this were true, then no one could ever authoritatively declare what is the truth, the way and plan of reality designed by our great Creator. Messed up lives are swimming in their experiential distortions concerning what is eternal truth. Let us not label such deviance as reality, nor fool ourselves into believing it is truth. We would be no better than Pontius Pilate and many others who pompously asked, "What is truth?".

In being a true believer in the one, true and living God, one must have a liberating and rock-solid conviction of the perfectness of this Creator/Sustainer/Savior. This One who is exalted above all is the sole possessor of the attributes of being all-knowing, all-present, and all-powerful. In His perfect wisdom He has chosen to impact upon this sphere of universal creation with the irreplaceable essence of truth. In this case this verity is not hamstrung with ideas and philosophies. It presents itself without error in the form of a Person. Its illustration to us earth creatures must be with an unapproachable dynamism. Rather than being steered insanely by philosophical proponents, truth can be nailed down in the life of the only One through whom this is possible. Out of God's stupendous mercy, we can now latch hold to the flawless exhibition and expression of truth in Truth himself, Jesus Christ, the only begotten of God.

Confronting The Maze

How do we grasp this truth in the midst of a fuzzy, misleading world which pulls at us in all directions? Jesus himself declared the mandate placed in and on Him by his Heavenly Father, "I am the Way, the Truth, and the Life".

(John 14:6) With this insurmountable place in all of creation, He was able to affirm that He was God's only access to the Heavenly Father and His heaven. With the magnificent awareness of this heavenly provision from our all-loving God, maybe one shortfall for us is failing to see ourselves as He sees us, with a redemptive heart and eyes. It is important to recall a little-recognized event in the life of Jesus. He was confronted by the rich young ruler who inquired about the criteria of inheriting eternal life. Jesus answered, and was informed by the young man that he had kept the commands even from his youth. The scripture said that Jesus looked on him and loved him, and gave him further instructions. Jesus knew he needed redemption, not reaction. (Mark 10:21) If He is so willing, this cries out for some faith on our part to believe inside that real victory, a cleansing, and liberation is there for our taking. God even rejoices and responds to merely a mustard grain of faith. How dramatically different this is from those in the world who believe that their god demands that they carry out unjustifiable and senseless murder! What contrast this dark god is compared to the One, true, living God, father of the Lord Jesus Christ, who brings light and awareness of His blessing. It is imperative that we open our hearts and spiritual ears to Him. Our foundation of faith is not based on well-meaning-but-insensitive legalists.

As Paul pointed out in Galatians and elsewhere, the only thing that legalism does is define right and wrong. It has no redemptive or restorative power, offers no hope or healing. As Paul described the law, if the law were our answer, then Jesus died in vain. The lost or backslidden person already knows his wrong and his guilt. Is it going to change him and her to keep throwing the law in their face? Hardly! They need a hope and a witness that there truly is a way out, and indeed that way is Jesus, not mere *churchianity*! Here the call is to the church, the saints, individually and gathered, to be the loving and redemptive salt and light to those both in torment and journeying in the fog. Drawing one into restoration is much more effective and lasting than trying to beat or lecture them into it. It is like the old adage about God in fishing for men, "You catch 'em; I'll clean 'em". There is so much darkness present which envelopes those who are inwardly crying out for our light as it displays Jesus.

We must remember, "Give as freely as you have received!" (Matt. 10:8)

Self? What Is Self?

In approaching the complex issue of sorting through the challenges of personal struggles, one is inevitably confronted with many familiar references to self.

Not only is this sometimes rather difficult, but its importance is amplified by the fact that usually the consequences and outcome of this search are so great. Scripture and life values haunt us with the need to experience the positive realization of self.

Somehow the word even seems dry and hazy. According to the American Heritage dictionary, self is described as the "the total, essential, or particular being of a person; the individual". Webster adds, "personality, character, individuality. An individual's consciousness of his own being or identity". The Greek word 'sauton' from Matthew 19:19 and elsewhere is translated as "thee, thine own self, thou, and thy self". According to this textbook approach, our self does include our mental, emotional, spiritual, and physical makeup. If this were not complex enough, this comprehensive being of our self is directed to love God with our totality. (Matt. 22:37)

The rest of this verse mandates that our response and interaction with others are to have the same connection, "and your neighbor as yourself". The first is primary to the unfolding of the second. This is because we are going to Love Himself in order to experience and share this essence. We begin to see that herein lies the key, catalyst, and genesis of self-love and other-love. Understand clearly that this is impossible to create and project on our own. Most persons attempt this, breaking some degree of sweat to "make things better, or religious". Though the intention may be honorable, the effort becomes counterfeit. If true and genuine love is evident, it has been passed down through Him, through Jesus. God in His wisdom must have reasoned from the beginning that if His only approach to His creation was that of exhibiting Himself as some big overbearing magistrate, He would have little chance of creating or sustaining its attention. Apparently He spoke vividly and clearly to His early prophets to benefit their understanding without developing the spiritual intimacy found in the New Covenant. This is not to say that some, as David, did not praise Him intently and seek a closeness. God the Father planned personal interaction and dynamic redemption in an unmistakable way by visiting us through His Son, Jesus Christ.

Filling The Blanks

His love for us is revealed in complete comprehensiveness in Jesus. He made our natures and created us with a need to be loved. God knew, notwithstanding any man who has let his heart turn to stone, that no one can really resist genuine love. Often man may only allow himself to taste of love sent his way, all the while keeping up his guard. But, he discovers that when this expression is authentic, he begins little by little to weaken his resistance, a journey of emerging trust. This is the self with all its stains and darkened memories beginning to sample that which can only fill the void within. Quite possibly he has been emotionally burned and is very mistrusting as in a marriage dispute. He will come nearer to accepting love and caring from a human who displays this kind of love than responding blindly to legalistic preaching. This particular type of love from the Greek would likely be *phileo,* a brotherly and friendship expression.

Here we are not talking about *eros*, demonstrating the erotic. Neither are we dealing with *storge*, pertaining to family. Nor are we considerting *agape*, the perfect and selfless love as from the Father. This reinforces the mandate for us *called-out ones* to be salt and light. An old saying says that "Your actions speak so loudly I can hardly hear what you're saying". This can reflect both positive and negative interaction. Another is similar, "I don't care how much you know until I know how much you care", setting the selfish ego in its rightful place. This is the critical juncture where the self can grasp what real love can be. This person can experience a genuine love when the giver is sharing that perfect love of Jesus with him. Only then will there be no hidden agendas, no ulterior motives. Another familiar saying declares that "You may be the only Jesus some person may ever see". Once we get our self out of the way, the Lord can use us to shine through to these struggling identities who have mostly experienced an unattractive self. This is why God is not looking for our ability, but our availability. The real secret is for these unfulfilled souls to discover they can live a victorious life because they encountered one who displays the Jesus they so desperately needed.

Free, I See

Those who latch onto this liberation begin to see their viewpoints and desires experiencing change. They emerge out of their shells to begin the voyage of truly caring about others. They sense that this is what they have been missing. They in turn are beginning to "Taste and see that the Lord is good". (Ps. 84:8) They begin to enjoy some light for their darkness, and soon experience the surprise that this good God is finally utilizing them. Loving "your neighbor as yourself" is becoming experiential. This love cleanses and heals in order for him to forgive, accept, and love himself, namely, in right-standing with him. Daylight dawns as he encroaches upon the realization of how God sees him. Self is no longer viewed as a problem, but really a blessing with great and liberating potential.

It is very important that as this understanding of a redeemed and victorious self begins to emerge, in his down-to-earth frankness with God he must take a first step for help. The first may be this genuinely loving person, this intercessor, that God has put in his path. The second calls for his heart-felt appeal to God to help him personally. The enemy of his soul and entire being, satan, will employ various means to discourage this restorative journey. This enemy will use any and every means at his disposal to bring deception and defeat. This man experiencing this healing must immerse himself in God's Word, especially the New Testament at first. The letters of the apostle Paul and others will encourage him, as in I John 1:9, and "the Spirit that is in you is greater that the spirit who lives in the world. (I John 4:4)

Tell It, With The Spirit

One will readily see the difference between just "Bible preaching" and anointed teaching. Quite often the first seems to be laden with harshness and legalism. Anointed teaching will instruct in holy living and faith, but also encourages and empowers. This new self, being liberated, needs to seek out anointed teaching whereby the Holy Spirit can move in and do victorious work. We recall the bumper stickers which said, "Be patient; God is not finished with me yet", and "Christian, under construction". The newly encouraged Christian has been bought and paid for, his plans laid out, and the work begun to demonstrate the beauty of the Builder for His tenant.

The person coming alive in the spirit will begin to exercise comparisons, such as standard *churchianity* contrasted with walking in and with the Spirit. God's Word declares, "wherever the Spirit of the Lord is, He gives freedom". (II Cor. 3:17) Conventional churches don't have to be a hindrance to spiritual growth, and indeed shouldn't be. Where saints are gathered, praise of God should be rendered, and the Word promulgated should be a ripe setting for growth in the spirit. The person seeking assurance, encouragement, and instruction in spiritual matters may find that institutionalism lacks the arena for personal progress. The agenda and motive of many churches dampens freedom and healing. When it comes to worshipping the Father and witnessing deliverance ministries, the person who wants to discover their relevancy is in great need of the touch and indwelling of the Spirit.

Just Trying To Love Others

I n most cases of those who struggle with self-degradation or unforgiveness, there seems to be a submerged unrest which lingers as if by design to rob one of peace. Defense mechanisms and coping skills are mustered and appear as if they will keep this monster at bay. For the most part, life experience seems to be workable. We have a tendency to justify our shortcomings because we can always think of others who appear to be worse than we. It must be clarified here, as by the premise of this book, that the answer is not to punish one's self. That is no answer at all. The rub here is that our thought patterns and the enemy of our souls tell us that we deserve it. That makes it seem acceptable. We shrug and say, "Why argue the point?"

Let it be understood here that the wounded soul is able to love, at least as he or she is able to grasp it. Imperfect and misdirected love is more prevalent than most are aware of. Jesus was cognizant of this which prompted Him to say, "If you love your father or mother more that you love me, you are not worthy of being mine" (Matt. 10:37) This is usually where the humanistic proud ones readily proclaim that there is nothing more important than loving one's children, or parents, or siblings, etc. They are usually quite assertive and even angry when declaring this viewpoint, then challenge their lifestyle. The appeal here is how noble this sounds. "Surely, no one can disagree with this". The damaged soul easily identifies with this viewpoint. The real issue is not that this premise is to be banished into outer darkness. Some good does come from trying to love others even with an insufficient love. The problem is attempting to redefine a heavenly experience with mere temporal expression.

Genuine Article

Real love is not an evolving essence as many think of 'monkey-to-man'. The Bible wakes us up by announcing that "For from within, out of a person's heart, come evil thoughts, sexual immorality, theft, murder, adultery, greed, wickedness, deceit, eagerness for lustful pleasure, envy, slander, pride and foolishness." (Mark 7:21,22) The word 'heart' here from the Greek word, kardia, means thoughts or feelings. Confusion often develops between possessiveness and self-giving, self-sacrificing love. It is truly not a matter of the flesh, but of the spirit. This fortifies the fact that, in order to love perfectly and deeply, the spirit must be in complete harmony with its Creator. Let it be understood that all persons are born with a human spirit whose design is to be made alive in God to reap oneness with Him eternally. This is pertinent when we find that the Bible states, "God is love". (I John 4:16) So, real love, either for self or others, gets its real and intended definition from God Himself, clearly demonstrated in and through His Son Jesus Christ. This is why I Corinthians 13 is so vivid and crucially important to clarify what love is, and its rightful place. It ranks above all else. Its design by Love Himself is to never be subordinated. This love is the only sort that, by the design of its Creator, fortifies and sustains life.

Slippery Ahead

Perhaps, then, if we are trying to love others mostly on the emotional level, we must learn how and where this falls short. Someone is always quick to point out that they know of some family which is very close-knit and appears to love each other more than some 'religious families' do. The visual assessment here is understandable. Where the problem exists is that those in this category demonstrating affection and even commitment are not truly alive in this God who is Love. They are ignorant of the fact that true and pure love isn't generated from instinct or emotion, but from Love Himself. He brings this about in the spirit of man, which is itself eternal. Unbelievers and CINO's (Christians In Name Only) have given themselves the credit. Though this type of love may not fall under the category of 'evil', it falls short of God, and His intentions and plan. This preoccupation with one's own goodness is precisely why God let His creations know, "Thou shalt have no other god before me". (Ex. 20:3) In scripture this fallacious habit is known as 'missing the mark', a biblical phrase for sin.

Spell It Out

It is appropriate now to render a comprehensive definition of the word 'love'. First, let us draw from the Hebrew in the Old Testament, In Leviticus 19:18 we find, "Thou shalt love thy neighbor as thyself". The commandments are ever-present as in Deuteronomy 6:5 which declares, "Thou shalt love the Lord thy God with all thy heart, with all thy soul, and all thy strength." In these the word 'love' is the Hebrew word 'ahab' which means to 'love as his own soul.' Those attempting to claim this expression as their own, yet living in godlessness, are concentrating on taking the credit.

In the New Testament *love* is recorded in Matthew 22:37-39. The same verses by Jesus in the original Greek manuscripts used the word 'agapao' which means to love with the idea of affectionate reference, prompt obedience and grateful recognition of benefits received. The associated word more familiar to the Christian public is 'agape' which talks about affection, benevolence, and even a love feast of charity. The American Heritage Dictionary describes love as 'an intense affectionate concern for another person'.

This short academic clarification is a foundational reference in understanding where authentic love integrates our own souls. This applies both to our love for others and our love/acceptance of ourselves. It may be appropriate here to clarify that this is not the same as our misuse of this word when admiring a dress, pet, or song, for instance. To desire to extend a love that counts as a valid expression calls for an inner cleansing that literally allows us to minister pure love to others, and be enveloped by that love simultaneously. As we have just learned, the yardstick includes loving one as his own soul. With an affectionate reverence, we are to be willing to obey Love as He leads, committing ourselves to demonstrate gratitude and an affectionate concern for another. Vital to such an effort is the knowledge that, even though we may not feel like the pure expression of love, our willingness to care will nonetheless bless and encourage someone.

Loving with this completeness accomplishes two vital missions. Yes, it gets across to others our caring for them. But, this is also coupled with getting outside ourselves. This is experienced as being loosed to let God's grace minister to us and through us. The prevalence of distraction and frustration is removed. Indeed, we are blessed to be a blessing! Only this will enable us to even love the unlovely, to truly be the instrument of God.

Crucial Decision

What we have found here is that true love is not mere emotion and feeling. What if God in John 3:16 limited himself to being 'so emotional about the earth that He gave His only begotten Son . . .'? Man's imperfection and grossness would cause God to be discouraged instantly. So, by what we learn in His Word, real and Holy love is, first of all, decision. This type of decision had to have been made before He set about creation. The act was too great, and the consequences too involving to attempt this undertaking lightly. Secondly, love is commitment. Jesus well understood this when He said, "Anyone who puts his hand to the plow and then looks back is not fit for the Kingdom of God" (Luke 9:62) His highest example was in completing the mission given Him by his Father. This commitment of love was to the cross and the redemptive sacrifice for all mankind.

Paul F. Allen

This is why we can answer our own question, "Why can't I just keep trying to love as I have been?" Our clumsy efforts cause a semblance of caring. If we analyze what we are involved with here, it is that highly valuable asset and offering from Him who is love. We dare not cheapen or minimize this incomparable blessing. It mandates our desire that we become His instruments of love. This is where we get fulfillment, and He gets the credit.

Does Monkey See?

For many decades or longer there has been an old adage which said *monkey see, monkey do.* It was a crude but effective way of explaining a distinctive characteristic of a person. It usually meant the subject person was merely a carbon copy of someone of close acquaintance, often a parent or sibling. More times than not, the reference was to negative behavior or expressiveness.

In trying to understand why one displays an empty or self-absorbed concept about their life might be because they may have been modeling themselves after a certain influential *teacher.* It could even be from a contemporary influencer who seemed to be stronger and *had it all together.* This could possibly be narrowed down to envy. Thus, we begin to see that this person's void was not filled with assurance, peace, hope or even love. Can we see how his life's journey is devoid of giving benefit either toward others or himself? Thus, our neighbor as ourself doesn't stand a ghost of a chance. Knowing and loving God gets derailed, and blessing others is largely out of reach.

Never Make It

The apostle Paul declared in I Corinthians 13 not only the value of love, but included the other gold nuggets of the believer's life which are faith and hope. One can usually observe hopelessness in a person in their conversation, isolation, and assuredly in their eyes. This can easily be compared to the appearance of the eyes of one filled with fear or terror. We can also see a difference in the eyes of one filled with joy and elation.

When one has arrived at that stage of hopelessness, virtually all assessments radiate negativity and despair. Profane expressions are frequently the fruit of such defeat. This is why Jesus said that our mouths reveal what our hearts are full of. (Matt. 12:34) These defeated ones will usually say, "Aw, to heck with it!", or "Ah, what's the use?" Often the *blame game* will rear its ugly head, which could stretch to the ends of the earth.

Finally, self-degradation sets in and they will utter, "I will never be able to do this" or "It's all my fault." Condemnation fills the void within, and amazingly, it all seems so logical! We hear, "Man, I'll never make it." The fruit of this preoccupation can often lead to self punishment, or escapism such as alcohol, drugs, and many other indulgences. The other might be climbing into one's hideout and becoming non-social. The Lord and His Word are the answer to this person in need!

The Law's After Us

As discussed, in the New Covenant the law is merely our instructor. It has no redemptive power in itself. The early Hebrews were given hundreds of laws and were expected to keep them. The New Testament clarifies that in breaking one, we are guilty of all. The defeated person, even within the Christian fellowship, can become burdened with the flaws in their lives, and wonder if they will ever beat the rap. They question, "Where is God in all of this?' Or, they may say, "I'm a Christian. Aren't I supposed to be walking in victory?' Then, inevitably they usually ask, "What have I done wrong? Will I ever please God?' Consequently they will conclude, "God must be mad at me because I make mistakes. I'll bet my dad, my teacher, my coach never goofed like I do."

This struggler needs peace and reassurance. Yet, paramount in his thoughts is the fact that somehow he has broken the rules. He deduces that this is what the whole issue is all about. Thus, we admit the law is necessary, yet never redeeming. It does what it is supposed to do, though never brings healing or joy. The law can seem vicious, but never victorious. It is so hard to live up to it, and that is what makes one feel so depressed. It is like the old saying, "You can't live with it, and you can't live without it."

There is no way anyone can play by all the rules, so that leaves us without hope. Could there possibly be any method to escape their demands and punishment? Most can identify with the apostle Paul's cry when he said, ". . . . who will free me from this life that is dominated by sin?" (Rom. 7:24) This was in recognition of his mistakes and faultiness. The issue which brought him to this dilemma was the law which revealed his shortcomings.

As mentioned elsewhere, a ransom or other demand is needed to set one free from their captivity. Our Creator God has always known this and has always desired to set satan's captives free. To do this He had to pay the price. However, He has never owed satan anything, so He did not pay him anything. To *pay* means to satisfy the demand for the purchase. If God bought us back from the clutches of judgment and death, He satisfied the demand He established which was necessary for this accomplishment.

The law levels demands at its subjects. Hopelessness arises because man can see no way to undo the mistakes, no way to keep from breaking the law. "Owe no man anything except to love one another, for he who loves another has fulfilled the law." (Rom. 13:8 KJV} Aren't we blessed with this provision?!

Yes-Way, Man

E ven Jesus said that He did not come to do away with the law, or the prophets. He did not come to destroy, but to fulfill. (Matt. 5:17) Here the word *fulfill* is from the Greek word *plero* which means to satisfy, to end by fulfilling the criteria. With this we see that the advent of Jesus the Messiah and His sacrifice on the cross fulfilled the demands. This was His appointment, and His alone. Thus, we can understand His declaration which said, "I am the way, the truth, and the life. No one can come to the Father except through me." (John 14:6) This is the foundation of the Gospel, the Evangel, the good news. The issue here is that we cannot make ourselves right with the all-righteous God by our own intellect or effort. Casting our focus on even saved but fallible men is an exercise in failure. If we were to follow them, we would understand *monkey see, monkey do.*

This brings us to the liberating truth. Rather than continuing to be a victim of the condemnation of the law, we become aware of the only way to the Father and His promises. We alone can't do it, so someone simply has to run to our rescue. How can he do this if he is merely another man as we? If Jesus is the one who alone absorbed the demands of the law for our sakes, then the law should no longer be a prime focus in our lives. Our attention then turns to this One who alone did satisfy all these demands for our sakes. As a result, what we begin to understand about our God and His Word is that our victory is handed to us on a silver platter!

This is where we understand the heavenly irony of victory through surrender. To receive the blessing of this God, this Savior, and His Word, our egos even with their burdens must step down from the throne. Surrender to Him ushers in His rightness and freedom. This is because He is on our throne, working miracles and affirming the love that we are made to receive and give.

Me? Love Others?

L ove in our existence is the one experience that generates positive miracles. Isolationism or anger often produce amazing results, but they are hurtful and negative. To get to this positive state of mind, Paul talks elsewhere in Romans (12:2) about being transformed by the renewing of our minds. This means we learn to think and act as our Creator desires and has designed. This transformation comes not from the world's philosophies, but from God's Word. And, it's more than mere intellect. The Holy Spirit of God is identified in scripture as our instructor. Therefore, the apostle again talks about Christ who searches our hearts and knows the mind of the Spirit. If anyone knows the issues of the mind, it is He.

So, to complete our true destiny in this cosmic creation, being in harmony with our Creator/Sustainer should be the goal and desire of all men. When this happens, the renewing of our minds beckons changing the spirit in us to be lovers, specifically, as givers. Existence as *takers* has revealed itself as merely self-serving. We get the revelation that some people we have admired and followed in the past who reveal their shallowness and emptiness. Their identity is not as those who bless and align themselves with Love himself.

Satisfy And Love

To be obligated to someone else puts one under legal burden, and tends to lead to unfriendly reactions. This person can either become angry or defensive. These are major roadblocks to freedom within, and happiness either with self or with others. There are two game plans when one owes something to another. Either the debtor attempts to remit whatever it takes to satisfy the issue, or they view the recipient as someone to avoid or even oppose. Needless to say, there is no peace and liberation in that.

Jesus told us that we would know the truth, and the truth would make us free. He even identified Himself as the Truth. If we follow His leading, peace and joy are the fruits. When one is filled with joy, it is hard to hold back. The revealer-of-wrongs, the law, no longer presents a burden. To re-emphasize, the apostle Paul gives the key when he instructs us that "If you love your neighbor, you will fulfill all the requirements of God's law." (Rom. 13:8) To know we are in a secure position with ourselves, with God, and with others, this is best demonstrated in the love and caring that we show. That nullifies all the errors pointed out to us by the law. Our victory is best demonstrated when we know we are forgiven, giving, and complete in our Christ.

Forgiveness Starts at Home

When we begin to get serious about our lives, their value and purpose, we begin to go through a mental and spiritual boot camp. It can be tough, but worth it. In ways it might be compared to a military recruit learning to defend himself in order to win the battle. At graduation his pride is bolstered by his appreciation of what he accomplished. Despite what some would have us believe, we are not really dummies. We go through life with the baggage of battling unworthiness and degradation, seemingly our lot in life without any real hope. We begin to wonder what 'real' is, and where the positive is. We punish ourselves by what we have learned repeatedly to accept. Shamefully, this may have come from others who are supposed to be the caring ones. We have been programmed to inner failure. To compensate, we do something erratic, overinflate our egos, or cave in completely. How sad and erroneous are these conclusions! Somehow we know there is something missing, causing us to feel that things are not quite right. Our egos and need for self-preservation prompts us to render our own solutions, the quicker the better. Future consequences are not evaluated at this point.

The issue that too few have discovered is that we have a heavenly construction which has on its blueprint a spiritual void. We are made that way for a purpose. Defensive personalities try their best to avoid yielding to this issue in their lives. Our Creator is most purposeful, but yet a gentleman by His design. That void is so that we find our meaning and destiny in Him. He is the only One who can fill it, and therein is the hitch. In His wisdom, when He designed us, our design included issues before us which seem only a hair's breadth of separation between mind and spirit. This plan of His mandates that to be whole and victorious now and forever, we must seek Him and His way. Seeking only the mental, self-centered way lands us into all kinds of hot water throughout our lifespan. But, if we are stubborn and choose our way, He will let us. He explains this choice of decisions in His Word which says, "There is a path before each person that seems right, but it ends in death." (Prov. 14:12)

A Hole In One, And All

We are allowed to let our emotions fill our void. This is so close to filling the void spiritually that it is rarely differentiated. We substitute emotional highs for spiritual wholeness, and where does it get us? Our inner void is yet empty because it is God's exclusive territory. Then, we pump up our egos like a mylar balloon and float them where everyone can see. This is how, in the soulish realm, we confirm and measure our importance. Particularly, if we can garner a small following of admirers, this is the counterfeit which massages our ego. Have we arrived? Hardly, for the same issue is at hand. This is not unlike the alcoholic who eases his anguish by *crawling back into the bottle* which got him there. This leads us to ask if we have conformed to the image of Christ. (Rom. 8:29) Have we let the Designer mold us as clay? The spiritual void remains, and this pressures us to substitute, to create counterfeits. But, there is also something more.

One of our main issues in finding out why we don't love or accept ourselves is to discover the fly in the ointment. We've made wrong choices, and we've substituted the artificial for the real. We don't like our jumbled mess. Many even rebel. It is like someone picking up a Christian tract only to tear it up in anger. We are similar to the alcoholic, until we get to that crucial point in our lives where we surrender to win. In this mode, in order to win we must compensate, usually unsatisfactorily. This is known in more intellectual circles as defense mechanisms. We constantly put up a front, or we are aware of the need to cover our tracks. Either experience is an inadequate path to follow. These fronts may be loud expressiveness, possession obsession, self-adornment to build up ourselves through appearance, continuing unrelentingly to be pre-occupied, or use a myriad of escapisms.

Go, Defense!

These issues can be boiled down to a single word which covers all the bases. This catalyst which causes so much deep and long-term injury is *justify*. When we act, speak, or even think in ways which are detrimental to ourselves or others, one of two things will necessarily follow. We could behead our pride and confess our mistake with repentance to God or the person we have affronted. This approach is the one which brings healing and a sense of victory. But, more often than not, with a problematic ego, people will seek to compensate by justifying their error with all manner of excuses in order to meet their ego needs. It is like the adage which says, "You can do one of two things with a lie. You can confess it and get it over and done with. Or, you must cover it with another lie." How deep and damaging can this go? It will fester like an untreated sore.

The Bind That Ties

Offense is that which brings about the need for forgiveness. This may be forgiveness from others, from God, or forgiveness of ourselves. We experience the inner pain of the excess baggage that we have been carrying around. It may have been seeded into us from a number of sources. Nonetheless we find it quite difficult to forgive ourselves for our stupid mistakes. Therefore it is high time that we now grasp some liberating revelation which will shed light on our journey to restoration.

In trying to face up to our sins and mistakes, we label ourselves as the lone operator in the driver's seat. "I should have known better. How can I ever clean this mess up?" How frustrated and helpless we feel. We need affirmation at this point rather than wallowing in another chapter in our history of failures. Definition of our person and spirit is very important at this juncture. Clear recognition is called for since an 'unseen enemy' lurks constantly. The prince of this earth, satan, is also known as the purveyor of darkness. (Eph. 6:11,12) By those willing to be influenced by him and his ways, his darkness appears to be as light. (Matt. 6:23) It seems like a logical path to follow. Yet, Jesus said how very great is that darkness! Most of us are fairly habitual persons, and find ourselves still rolling in our repetitive patterns, only to be derailed. For those not belonging to God in a saved relationship, this derailment appears acceptable, and normal fare. They create their own comfort zone which indeed misses the true journey which was willed by the Creator. Satan needs only to spend little time with them.

However, for those who are in a born-again relationship with God and yet don't feel or appear as overcomers, understanding is sorely needed. God paid too high a price to simply let a saint slip from His grasp. In God we have our true Master, our eternal Master. Jesus once taught about the fallacy of trying to serve two masters. Though that reference was teaching about a focus on riches, the issue and principle are the same. Knowing this, we begin to cry out, "Why am I still a dummy, a failure, etc.?" We must remember that by biblical definition we are a spirit, we have a soul, and we live in a body. Though our computerized memories continue to render torment, some negative input is promoted by the opportunist, satan. Other emotional and spiritual pain is experienced because of uncleansed and unhealed torment patterns. These stressful flashbacks of old patterns of our sin should never take their toll. God's Word is the solution! "Forgetting those things which are behind and reaching forth to those things which are before, I press toward the mark of the prize of the high calling of God in Christ Jesus." (Phil. 3:13 KJV) As an example we can only presume Jesus' debilitation during His temptation experience in the desert. With God's Word He defeated the enemy with heavenly resistance. (Jas. 4:7)

Certainly, if there are issues which we can readily deal with, such as unforgiveness, then we must pursue the issue and get it behind us. Blameshifting is never good nor a solution. It lowers us to the level of defeat. We must realize that unforgiveness breeds anger, a measurable negativity to our being and relationships. Feelings of hopelessness arise because amid the virtually unsolvable issues, we feel like we've been mastered. Of course, as we have established, we have only one Master.

Thus, our experience of torment is from external attempts to control our lives. Knowing the truth makes us free. (John 8:32) Only those living in deception, deviation, and lies will fear the truth. They often fly into rage which is merely a display of defensiveness. The ugly picture here is that our enemy wants us captive, never free, never victorious, never an over-

comer. The insecure victims try to run from, ignore, or drown out their troubling issues. The believer must realize and affirm that this external mastering attempt is not final, and has no real authority. Therefore, let us not feed the monster. We have the authority as Jesus did in his temptation experience to firmly declare the Word of God back at this enemy. He cannot stand it. He must flee. The true believer has the authority to put away fear and real discomfort which comes from the enemy of our souls. We recall the time Jesus called his apostles together and "gave them power and authority to cast out demons and heal all diseases." (Luke 9:1) This is our gift and blessing. After all, "the Spirit who lives in you is greater than the spirit who lives in the world." (I John 4:4)

Failure Or Forgiveness

A nother live issue which seems to plague many, including believers, is the oppression of failure, constantly reinforced by the pressure to perform. This comes from others and even standards we have placed on ourselves. Though it is a positive process to reach higher and set goals, most of the oppression comes from negative motivations and pressures. The fruit of this weight is usually detrimental to hope and possibilities, definite at odds with righteous living. The problem exemplifies that we can become confused between actual guilt and pseudo-guilt. This is where truth about God's forgiveness and redemption reigns triumphantly over burdens which cloud our restoration. We are mandated to recognize that when the pressure comes from ourselves or others to measure up, we must clearly face it if we are to bring positive results or merely negative influences from the grudge factory. Even well-meaning acquaintances can heap counter-productive pressure upon us. We hear rather self-righteous phrases like, "Doesn't the Bible tell you such-and-such?" That is known as truth (or maybe half-truth) without wisdom, which is a term signifying how one uses knowledge. Or, they may say, "Your brother (father, preacher) doesn't believe that way." Or, "You need to spend more time in prayer (Bible study, etc.)" Again, possible truths, but without wisdom and heart. This is where *good news* doesn't really sound so good.

Forgiveness of others and forgiveness of ourselves is the catalyst for the healing and victory that God has for us. He gets no glory in our sickness or defeat. Where He is glorified is in the victory we experience because of what He has done, is doing, and is going to do based upon His Word. This is what you can believe, because in Him, "You will know the truth, and the truth will set you free." (John 8:32)

There is another added bonus pertaining to the experience of forgiveness. Jesus said, "But a person who is forgiven little shows only little love." (Luke 7:47) Conversely we can conclude that great forgiveness reaps great love. Indeed, this definitely refers to our forgiveness and that of others. Most will say this is a decision from the mind. But it is deeper than this.

Redemptive acts are instigated from the heart, the spirit of man. What freedom it brings! Yet, it is also equally relevant to our forgiveness of ourselves. God tells us with promise that, "But if we confess our sins to him, He is faithful and just to forgives us and to cleanse us from every wrong." (I John 1:9) Forgiveness and cleansing; what more can we ask for? And, as established, there is no further attempt at negative mastering over our lives, because we are firmly established in the One and true Master.

We may truly dislike our lives and our history. God's mandate for us, lovingly as He has taught and shown, is that forgiveness be experienced and recognized in the light of the healing and liberation it brings as it opens floodgates. Self no longer becomes a stumbling block. God's Spirit is released to bring about magnificent things in and through us.

More Than Half Way

Most of us really enjoy those times when we were shown some grace, some extra favor to meet a pressing need. Maybe we were coming up a little short in meeting that need or challenge, or someone knew we needed a boost of encouragement nonetheless. It not only provides much needed relief, but it makes us feel so positive like taking a deep breath of fresh air. It builds our faith.

We witness mountains becoming mere *mole hills*. This brings to life the liberating experience of hope. The taste of new hope is second to hardly no other feeling or experience. Discovering that our attentive God wants us to walk in victory and freedom is just such an experience. We who have been burdened with excess baggage so long can look forward to being met with hope vivid enough to blow away those clouds.

There are two main keys to the assurance of God's effort to meet us more than half-way. This reminds us of when the Prodigal Son in Luke 15:11 decided that even servanthood at home was better than what he was going through. Though willing to crawl back and win favor, he was met with a great surprise. The father in his compassionate and redeeming love saw him at a great distance and was not willing to wait. He hurried to him with uncontrollable joy and love which moved him to roll out the red carpet. This familiar story illustrates these two keys. They are His unconditional love and His faithfulness.

In the sales field, if one is to be successful, two factors must be in force and active at all times. These ingredients are being consistent and persistent. The very same principle is a dependable offering of our God towards us. Where we are concerned, these two ingredients are driven by this love and faithfulness. He cannot help Himself. It is His nature. Amazingly, the same fruits are seen in the lives of God's people who are triumphant in their walk with Him. They are living lives of triumph and service because they are consumed with the nature of love and faithfulness. They are both consistent and persistent. Underscoring all this is their faith, that thing without which we cannot please God. (Heb. 11:6). This illustrates how useless mere religion is, designed only to make us feel religious.

Many years ago the author was on the staff of a church which invited a somewhat notorious ex-con to speak. He had been in many of the largest prisons in the nation, even rubbing elbows with infamous thugs like Machine Gun Kelly. He was incarcerated for several years for many felonies. As his 'tour' progressed, he gambled a lot to pass the time. He got into a heated argument with another inmate over a card game, and killed him. This assured him a journey to death row and solitary confinement. While there with nothing to do, he was handed a Bible. To beat the boredom, he began reading. Indeed God met him more than half way through His Word. This prisoner repented of all his sin and accepted Christ as both Lord and Savior.

To make a long and complicated story short, he became a powerful witness to the guards and finally to other prisoners. The God of miracles effected his parole which released him from prison. The key factor in this complete change was his mother's endless prayers. In speaking to this church body, one of his main statements was, "Don't ever let anyone tell you prayer doesn't work. My mother prayed for me for 30 years." Indeed, God's love and faithfulness works because He is sovereign. Yes, her prayers were consistent and persistent. Our Lord's great delights are to see us exercising faith, and to answer our prayers. Sadly enough, most people, even believing Christians, have grown up with a mindset that life ultimately is a composite of good and evil. We justify ourselves into believing that all is okay or that we will never make it, so what is the use?

It is at this point that we need to discern something about God's love. The immature viewpoint is that He is that good old guy in the sky, and loving us is just His job. It is equally erroneous to assume that we earn or merit His love because we are not really bad, or He is an old softee. Thus He considers our good works and attitudes as sufficient to win over his kindness to us. Often the mumbling begins here with, "That's the kind of God I believe in, or else forget it." Thus, his misery remains. For us to be secure and move ahead in our faith and understanding, we must accept that God's immeasurable love comes our way because He himself has committed this great love simply and only because He made this quantum decision. He alone decided to love His creation, to be attentive to these eternal souls and spirits. In truth we can scarcely grasp the depth of such a decision, such love. Being omniscient, all knowing, God exercised His marvelous wisdom in not setting himself up for heartbreak by exhibiting only a temporal love. This is the flawed expression of most of humankind, understanding and demonstrating a love primarily for the human person, putting all their eggs in this one basket. Our Lord knew better than this. Indeed He cannot help but care about His handiwork, but has so made us with an eternal spirit which is His prime focus. And His *more than half way* love included the means, Jesus Christ, whereby we can be redeemed back to Him from our sinful alienation, having been misled, being rebellious, or both.

Let's understand this churchy term 'redeem'. Basically, it means to buy back, or satisfy the demand. In years past, retailers were known for issuing stamps for the amount of purchase. The buyer would then fill books with them, and when many were collected, would take them to a 'redemption store'. The store would then 'buy them back' in exchange for merchandise. The stamps satisfied the demand for whatever it took to obtain the merchandise. Thus, Jesus Christ has satisfied the demand of the law whereby we can be restored to our all-righteous God. Indeed, this is the core of the Good News! This magnifies the mandate for walking and growing in the Spirit.

We see that He has made the incomparable decision to love us with an eternal love. Now, the next decision is ours. We must follow through with the decision to let Him heal us. Many have been the physically afflicted who yet glorified Him, letting the light of the Lord shine through them. The author worked along side a polio victim of many years, bound to a wheel chair. Yet, she radiated the Lord within. Handicap was only in the body. This is why Jesus addressed the crippled man with the pertinent healing priority, the forgiveness of his sins which was the cure for his main obstacle. Of course, Jesus did the physical healing to the dismay of the critics on hand. In his defeated mindset, a victim hides in his dilemma in fear of uselessness and failure. Willfully choosing to tolerate our dilemma robs us of victory and freedom, and renders no glory to God. He is glorified when we are overcomers and "overwhelming victory is ours through Christ, who loved us." (Rom. 8:37) God's overall plan for His creation is more than merely winning the *heavenly reward*. A conqueror in a battle can only and merely win if that is all he chooses. But, *more than a conqueror* takes the spoils and enjoys the bounty. Consequently, we are blessed to be a blessing.

One of the greatest roadblocks to humankind is the plague of rejection. It can start at any stage of life, but predominantly in the early years. The main instruments of rejection seem to be family and close acquaintances, though not limited to these. Sadly, even some preachers and teachers do their fair share of condemnation. Without running the gamut of how this takes place, the more damaging issue is that we begin to internalize these assessments, and all too soon find ourselves believing these distortions about who we are, or the reality of our worth. This involves misplaced or undue trust in those spewing this mental onslaught.

Jesus clearly understood all of this, leading him to assert that "You will know the truth, and the truth will set you free". (John 8:32) Herein lies our mandate for oneness with Christ Jesus, who is Truth. What can we expect? Freedom! Liberty from heavy burdens and condemnation. Free to live, to be, and serve! The apostle Paul even reinforces this by saying that, "There is now no condemnation to those who are in Christ Jesus". (Rom. 8:1) Condemnation's judgment is that it is a negative tool, not utilized to bring freedom and wholeness.

We must not allow ourselves to live behind the lie of defeat. It did not come from your Heavenly Father who condescended to send His Son to bring us complete truth and victory. God's dream and vision for us is realized in grasping His plan for each and every one of us. Can you imagine the Creator of all things and all ages to shortchange His highest creation with no plan? He paid too high a price for us to flail about like a fish out of water. He is not giving up on His plan, anywhere. He is not giving up on us. All it takes is pouring your heart out to the Creator/Sustainer as afore mentioned. Couple that with thanksgiving, exercising faith, which truly pleases Him. This is where you experience having the "mind of Christ". (I Cor. 2:16) Indeed, this is where we discover the reality that we "can do everything with the help of Christ who gives me the strength I need." (Phil. 4:13) Constantly affirm aloud and privately to Him that "So if the Son sets you free, you will indeed be free." (John 8:36) He has given the Holy Spirit to bring you to this victory.

What about the issues that are yet unsettled in your life? The great assurances we have seen are no substitute for confession and repentance. But once this is done, cling to I John 1:9 as your anchor. "But if we confess our sins to him, he is faithful and just to forgive us, and to cleanse us from every wrong." Then, move on in Him. Don't be surprised if the father of lies, satan, tries to undermine you to revert back to your old self. We already know he is the "accuser" (Rev. 12:10) And, we also know that "there is someone to plead for you before the Father. He is Jesus Christ, the One who pleases God completely." (I John 2:1) He intercedes for us to affirm that we are forgiven and thus are in right-standing with the Father. To be in right standing with a person means you will be confident in their presence, not overcome with fear of mistreatment.

There is no hindrance between you and God. Trusting in this complete miracle, walk out the rest of your life letting no past issue be a hindrance to your ability to love, or forgiving and accepting yourself. Onward Christian soldier!

Sin? What Sin?

This generation seems inundated with persons whose philosophies want to challenge any sense of personal infraction or responsibility to higher authority. The ego's drive is to display the intellect which can challenge the right of any one or system which wants to limit unbridled freedom. What they will not admit is that this kind of expression is often costly or injurious to someone else, currently or in its unfolding. When laws are countered, it is commonly called *breaking the law.* This is an inaccurate term, probably stemming from Moses' first descent from the mount only to find his people worshipping a golden calf. This is when he broke the inscribed tablets. He returned to receive another set.

What we need to understand is that though the physical instrument was broken, the spirit and intent of the law was not. So, we really don't break a law. We are attempting to break its hold on us. In biblical terms this is known as sin. The New Testament talks about it as *missing the mark*. The mark in this instance is a statute or expectation which is to be our target's center. God's intent is that it is for our own good regardless of our primary reaction to its advent. Any collision between our minds and God's law or any just law doesn't break the law. The damage isn't to the Author or it source, but to the one who causes the infraction. This is due to the inner battle. Repeated continuously, it dulls the impact on soul and spirit, proving that it is more than mere data.

The Repeater

By the same token, any law without godly wisdom merely becomes detrimental to those to whom they pertain. For instance, if a parent is obsessive-compulsive, they might engender paranoia in a child who is afraid of many normal things. It is a taught law, but anything but beneficial to the child. Wisdom would point one to truth rather than overbearing obsessions. According to our Creator, we are blessed with an avenue to redemption and forgiveness. Mere legalism has its answer in the Redeemer, Jesus Christ. When one is over-saturated with legalism and shielded from hope, social and spiritual paranoia is the likely result. The nature of human creation cries out for hope, rightness and victory. When a person is raised without the wisdom and Word of God, they will be taught rules, some values orientation, and a self-serving preoccupation. When confronted with general public values, to circumvent the rules, they will resort to the well-known tool of justification. This usually leads to covering one lie with another. This is the sure roadblock to healing and victory.

Turn To The Right

For one to begin making decisions and responses which seem to be right, the real issue involved is the source of the guidelines. For a person to be righteous, the meaning is that he or she is in right standing with their Creator/God who is in complete right standing with Himself. This means that He is perfect wholeness, perfect holiness, perfect in authority. On these grounds He is mistake-free. A God like this in his purity is not subject to nor utilizes trial-and-error. His plans and His implementation are perfect. This Supreme Being is always right, always secure. Perfect worship must be voluntarily responsive, something from the heart! "It is not that we loved Him, but that He first loved us." (I John 4:19 KJV) Mere legal obedience is not acceptable. This smacks of a type of puppetry. If He is this pure in intent, it is inconceivable that He would burden His creation with a sense of defeat or uselessness. A righteous God is incapable of such frailty.

What About Religion?

What we find here is a person who is short of both Godly wisdom and relationship. He is one of the many who have put more faith in worldly values and assessments. A person like this may have been programmed by a well-intentioned mentor who also came up short in God's wisdom and relationship. This is better known as *religion*. Here our person in need has yet to learn that our God is not interested in religion. It was the religious ones who forced murder upon His Son. Religion can be anything focused upon or habitually committed to. This means it can be good or bad, deep or shallow, self-giving or self-serving. The prevalent error is to refer to Christianity as a religion. Maturing Christians need to know and affirm that our way of belief is, in fact, a Person and the way revealed by this Person. To call it a religion may be easy, but erroneous nonetheless. The true key is relationship. It is the real difference!

Real And Unreal

The self-abasing person who struggles to show love lives an impaired life. What he has discerned is less than complete or accurate. He feels bad about himself and usually about others. If he weighs his effectiveness in loving others by how much he loves God, he may find himself weighed in the balances and found wanting. Because of the lack of spiritual growth and wholeness, he will interpret this as sin in his life. Yet, this condition robs him of a victorious walk with his God and God's people. The value of repentance and forgiveness is incalculable. As mentioned, there are two things which are to be done with sin. Confess it, and get it over with. Or, try to hide it by covering it with another lie and sin. The former is liberation. The latter is enslavement and a compounding of guilt.

Our confidence comes from the fact that God loves us with an indescribable love, so much that He provides for our victory. The issue is not limited to real sin and guilt. Often spiritual and mental paranoia can plague a person because he/she was raised with negative programming. To discipline and rear a child with God-led influence is one thing. But, to destroy a child's sense of worth with destructive treatment is definitely detrimental to a person's self concept. If he sees and experiences godly love in his formative years, then he is most likely to know how to share that love. He will be more likely to live a godly life by regeneration and following God's Word. As he grows into loving God with his whole heart, he consequently learns the value and joy of loving others. Scripture affirms, "Godliness leads to love for other Christians, and finally you will grow to have genuine love for everyone." (II Peter 1:7)

The issue of the sin challenge in this modern age is amplified by our media, entertainment, and airways. Not only will multiplied temptations arise, but they are amply joined by false and misleading values. The tricky catalyst of misdirection to unholy choices and actions is the fact that they seem so logical, or they fit logically as the social norm of the day. Nothing very unusual, so it must be okay. This sounds a lot like a teenager's ploy, "But, they're all doing it!" We are exhorted to be "to let God transform you into a new person by changing the way you think." (Rom. 12:2) Transformed by what, and to what? Be influenced by what is popular or generally accepted? The Word of our all-righteous Creator is our answer. Indeed, we recall the biblical affirmation, "I have hidden your word in my heart, that I might not sin against you." (Psalm 119:11) The word *hid* is also translated protect, esteem, and lay up. To say the least, it is an internalization into the sanctuary of our being. This means that this Word of wholeness and victory secures us, and blooms heartily when it is needed. This is the display of freedom when one becomes an overcomer in Christ. Though not vaporized, sin loses its control. It is no longer master.

It's A Void!

Because of our eternal blueprint by our Creator, He forms us to be victors, yet vulnerable. This is because we are designed to come to Him as our supply, and not pursue fallible counterfeits. Our God allows substitutional pursuits and preoccupations because He is the perfect gentleman. He allows us to make our own choices, waiting on our transformation from being self-centered to being Christ-centered. This alone is when our choice will be His choice, that of filling the redeemed life.

To fill something means there has to be room or space which can be filled. By definition a space or void can be filled with virtually anything. If it is filled with waste, the results will be negative and deteriorating. This is a verity in both the material and spiritual realms. We are all familiar with the axiom of one bad apple in a barrel. When a person's inner, God-designed void invites or allows damaging input, it affects other areas of values and decisions. This is the choice which engenders sin and rebellion.

The answer to prevent or overcome the fruits of this invitation is making a victorious decision, one in accord with the Creator. This is His design, that He and His living Word fill this void. He is not impressed with our intellect. He isn't wanting our suggestions and excuses. God's deepest desire is that none should perish. (II Pet. 3:9) Letting His creation be deceived is not His plan either. Things get right when He is the filler of our need. Sin is no longer in control. The Holy Spirit becomes our guide and our strength. He leads us to love, laughter, victorious living!

For Crying Out Loud!

Clearly most of us understand the release we sense when we allow ourselves to cry as a certain occasion presents itself. It's a built-in blessing. Jesus was observed as weeping over the grieving of others when His friend Lazarus died. Sadly, some will even use the experience to manipulate others in order to gain selfish ends. Others have built up walls and a hardness of heart as to be devoid of shedding tears, thinking they are a sign of weakness. Yet, there are those who will unwittingly cry in fits of temper and rage. It is almost amusing to recognize that the tears themselves are neutral, taking no sides one way or the other. The heart of the matter is indeed the heart!

Additionally, crying doesn't limit itself to opening up the tear ducts. It exhibits itself as a yearning from deep within a person, usually over a highly sensitive situation. Jesus expressed his deep concern over Jerusalem which would not respond to the love and message that He brought. (Luke 13:34) This may be referred to as *crying out*, whether tears are shed or not shed. This is usually where the yearning for peace, help, and answers is in a desperation mode. On occasion some have felt driven to believe that suicide or revenge is the only answer. Most have experienced dire stress at some time in their lives, some at multiple times. Those who live behind defensive walls are missing a real blessing, human and spiritual.

It's In The Book!

Crying out is exhibited many times in the Bible. In the 34th chapter of Psalms, the psalmist David explains that, "The Lord hears His people when they call to Him for help. He rescues them from all their troubles." (v. 17) The righteous here are those who are in right standing with God. They need not hold back, finding precious accessibility to the Creator, the Sustainer and Savior of all. The Hebrew word for *cry* here, inasmuch as the Old Testament was written in Hebrew, means to shriek or cry out. This is because it is from within our innermost being. The need is very great, and we seem helpless and hopeless. The deepest call of being is trumpeting out to our Helper. This verse also declares that He delivers them out of trouble in response to this shrieking from the heart. From the original recordings, this term *delivers* is interpreted as "defend, pluck, preserve, rescue, and save". This is the only acceptable and valid response we crave in our crying out from the pain.

In the 10th chapter of Mark, the New Testament tells about a time when a blind man heard that Jesus was passing his way. He cried out to Jesus, but he was rebuked by the crowd. Yet, he was desperate and could not let this unique opportunity slip away. So, he cried out all the more. How beautifully the God-man Jesus responded and healed him, meeting him at his point of need. The New Testament meaning of *cry* from the original Greek means to 'scream, shriek, and exclaim'. This is confirmation that God is not merely aware of our circumstances, but He looks on the heart, the spirit man. He knows all about us, much more than we are aware on our own, yet loves us with that deep, unconditional love nonetheless. He is a responder to the outpouring of the heart. Compare this with uncaring, contemporary god-images which influence their followers simply to promote themselves. For example, it is dishonest for one to declare that he feels our pain when the bottom line is the promotion of self.

There was an occasion when the author and his wife, after attending a worship service, had a surprising encounter with a young man who was psychologically bound with worry, and desired someone to help. The compulsion was so intense that his chatter took no rest. His mindset was to find that magic pill to ease his pain and struggle. We soon realized that no mere words were sufficient, so we gave him the answer that would lead him in his climb back to peace and wholeness. We instructed him in his crying out to God to begin continuous praising. When his mind and soul seemed overwhelmed with anxiety, confusion, and self-condemnation, he was immediately to begin praising God, praising Jesus. Nothing else. The scripture says, "With my mouth will I make known thy faithfulness." (Ps. 89:1 KJV) He was not to beg, wail, moan or argue. Our mandate, lining up with God's Word, was to just praise God, continuously. We have the precious promise that the Lord "Inhabits the praises of Israel (His people)." (PS. 22:3 KJV) This is where God shows himself as Deliverer, the Provider of the peace that passes all understanding.

Bringing It Home

The author has first hand knowledge of this pit of despair, and of God's deliverance. In his late 20's he went through a nervous breakdown, yes, even while being a pastor. He went through months of intense medical treatment and was released without returning to the professional ministry at that time. To abbreviate many events, one day while working in a warehouse he was mentally and emotionally overwhelmed and believed that he was relapsing to his former condition. In panic, he felt like running. He believes without a shadow of a doubt that he heard God's voice in his inner ear say, "Enter into thy closet, and when thou hast shut the door, pray to thy Father in secret, and He shall reward thee openly". (Matt. 6:6 KJV) The only closet he could find was the bathroom. Once inside he quickly knelt by the lavatory and cried out, "God, I don't want to go back to the hospital, but if that is your wish, then I'll go. But, I need your help right now". He left the bathroom and began filling orders mechanically. After a very few minutes he realized he was enveloped in peace. No turmoil, no fear, no shaking! God indeed is merciful! He is a responder!

Our mission is to pour our hearts out. It doesn't have to be religious sounding or preachy. Heaven forbid! It is a matter of pouring yourself out to Him in all honesty. Even if doubts have arisen, He gladly responds to such a simple appeal as, "God, if you're there, please help me!". Set your mind and heart to prohibit your past from robbing you of the blessing that is yours. God's Word exhorts us, "forgetting the past and looking forward to what lies ahead." (Phil. 3:13) Actually, awareness of our past can be a positive sign of our longing to be right, whole, and accepted. Our Father is very aware of that longing. Counterfeits to real healing are short-lived. That is because our true identity is that we are a spirit, we have a soul, and we live in a body. The wholeness of the spirit man is the primary concern of our all-powerful, all-present, all-knowing God, Jehovah Rapha, the Lord our Healer.

They're Demonstrating out There!

While we may be quick to internalize unpleasant thoughts which make us disappointed with ourselves, maybe it would be appropriate to examine ourselves with a little more objectivity. The problem with a negative mindset is that it all seems to be so logical. Somehow it just seems to make sense that our self-examination highlights our faults, failures and misgivings. This is augmented with a constant awareness of what we feel we could and should have become or accomplished. So, we conclude, what is there to feel good about? Loving neighbor as self doesn't quite seem workable with such a low self-opinion. We ask what we have to give that is worth having and that is attractive and acceptable to anyone else.

One By One

We need only to disregard others' opinions and discern the academic definition of love. After all, this is apparently at the top of the list with our Creator God. It is not only something pleasurable and encouraging to experience, but by design it is something to be given to others, even beyond family. Without question, a sure sign of love is caring. An old adage makes us reflect on this. "You can give without caring, but you can't care without giving". How many times have virtually all of us offered some item or even intangible acknowledgment largely because we felt obligated, or in an effort to avoid criticism?

Must we always feel emotionally charged when caring enough to give? Probably not. We can surmise that when Jesus turned water to wine, He was probably not overwhelmed with tender emotion. At least, we don't detect this in scripture. What He did was respond to a need simply and emphatically because He cared. This caring was love that arose from a desire to bless. When we care enough to bless someone or some worthy cause, it emerges not from evil or mechanical display, but from the essence of love. This is why preoccupation with being just a *faith person* is not good enough. In the book of James we find that having faith without the application of love, called works, is called worthless. (Jas. 2:15-18)

Before we shortsell ourselves by questioning whether we have no love to give, we need to admit that we have experienced many occasions where we displayed caring spontaneously because we knew it was timely, best, and needed. Undergirding all this demonstration of caring is the source affirmed in God's Word, namely, "God is love". (I John 4:8) If we go so far as to confess that we are His because we have united with Him through the Lordship of His Son, Jesus Christ, then this is where genuine love, caring and compassion abide in us. This caring is one expression that all can acknowledge as emerging from us, however clouded with conflicting emotions.

A Closer Look

Focus is one of those decisions which demands discipline. The real key is for everyone to keep "a pure eye" (Matt. 6:22), firmly acknowledging our God as Master of all. He is the Author of all true love. That essence abides in us although we may not realize it. Our mistake is discrediting that miracle which is a gift from Him. Many today who don't adhere to the knowledge of Him get involved in demonstrating a human attentiveness on their own.

We look at them and their families and conclude that, yes, they seem to be exhibiting love. They lack the understanding that this is the merciful implantation of the Creator in order to bless His creatures. How indescribably great is our God who can speak creation into being and inundate it with His greatest expression, His love! Of course, His own focused desire is that everyone come into union with Him through the Lord

Jesus Christ. So, we are clearly coming up short by crucifying self which is permeated with His righteous love. This gives us proper perspective concerning our focus in the living of these days.

Let us ask ourselves a challenging question. When our heavenly Father views us, would our perfect and righteous God misuse His efforts by limiting His focus to only the negative especially when He sees His born-again children as righteous? This would be a clearcut example of a judgmental and legalistic dictator. Sadly, this is the perspective of those who cannot accept the good. All the flaws cloud their vision. Oh yes, to them it seems justifiable. The problem is that they did not get this from our Lord. "God did not send His Son into the world to condemn it, but to save it. (John 3:17) Indeed, love by caring and giving is the demonstration of the presence of God throughout all of society.

It's Who Gets The Blame

Remember the old pep talk which starts, "It's not whether you win or lose . . ."? The sub-topic title above seems to have replaced "it's how you play the game". Our soul and spirit are the real key here. The soul is that intangible part of our being made up of the mind, will, and emotions. Don't we find it amazing how many are quick to name the blame using just these three elements?

Many are the theories as to why our minds become derailed into a negative, defensive, defeated mindset. Maybe we can boil it down to three major influences. First, early in our adolescent lives our genes play a major part in our formation, coupled with critical inferences in upbringing by our parents or guardians, joined by lack of reinforcement. Later, depending on our circumstances at home, school, and work, we may have been bombarded with degrading, vengeful condemnation which piled on the mental/emotional burdens. Lastly, that opportunist, satan, makes sure we get the worst end of the deal with degenerating relationships and bad programming. He feeds us false information and half-truths to steer us from our God-intended life. Unlike God, satan hides his identity while revealing himself as nothing but a taker, never as a giver of truth, wholeness and goodness.

This, of course, is because he has none of these three virtues in him. What is his key card? He makes it all sound so logical, enough that we might begin to really believe some of it. He feeds the soul which is starved of truth and beauty.

Key To Liberation

Realizing how we have gotten so far off-base, what foundation do we have when challenged by satan's wiles? In God's word to us, we find that "Anyone who wants to come to him must believe that there is a God and that he rewards those who sincerely seek him." (Heb. 11:6) To declare this puts us on a redemptive and restorative path. Somehow our minds and spirits have to experience a change in order for us to understand and become a true demonstrator of victory. It is ours to have! God's plan is not to hold back, but to give. He is glorified in our victory, not in our defeat.

God our Creator knows more about us than we ourselves. When a transformation is needed, He does not leave us out in the cold. Through the apostle Paul, God let the Roman Christians know that many needed to go through a change for their own sake as well as the sake of the Kingdom. In his letter to them he instructed believers to "let God transform you into a new person by changing the way you think." (Rom. 12:2), that we may be able to discern the will of God. As far as our physical and mental perspective is concerned, health and wholeness is His will. We find this in I Peter 2:24, III John 2, the ministry of Jesus, and many times elsewhere in both the Old and New Testaments. Without exception this must be the desire of all who have become His children through their faith in Jesus Christ.

Yes, *inquiring minds want to know*: with what are our minds to be renewed? To be re-newed implies that they were new at one time, namely, that they were new creatures in Christ Jesus. (II Cor. 5:17) Apparently something took place in the human journey which distorted, weakened, and possibly debilitated the mind enough that mental and spiritual surgery was imperative. Mere good advice assuredly falls short of what is really needed. A transformation is the only answer. The validity of the necessity here is made clear because only by this cleansing and healing can we determine what God wants of us. Nothing takes a higher priority. Finding this righteous plan for our lives is the very foundation of peace and belonging we desperately need. The product of this renewing refreshes our viewpoint on life and self. Then and only then do we find our acceptance before God and with ourselves.

Getting The Field Ready

To consider rejuvenating the people we contact, referred to as "neighbors", so that they will be open recipients is an overwhelming thought. That is not our responsibility. The field that does need cleansing and preparation is our very own lives. Our self-abasement and reluctance to bless others might stem from the rocks and briars that clutter our soul and spirit. They keep us from envisioning any good, any fruitful yield possible for us or others. With sinful spiritual and mental debris steering our lives, we make our lives as a field whereby our Lord is unable to bless, reveal, and bring forth righteous fruit. Loving self and others is the foundational fruit which undergirds everything else. No substitute can be found in mere professionalism, cunning, or intellectualism.

No Rub-A-Dub

Understand that the recognition of these issues is not a message of condemnation, but a call to enable us to become that "new creation in Christ." (II Corin. 5:17 KJV) With these burdens off our lives, we become free to live out His desire. The liberating factor about confronting sinful clutter is that it is ours to experience. This simple exercise requires that we admit our sin and rebellion to the Lord. We need not waste time and effort trying to clean up ourselves first. We have all tried this and failed. Nor should we attempt to excuse ourselves. He knows all about us, yet loves us nonetheless Again, this forgiveness which brings about cleansing is His doing. He through Christ Jesus puts us right with Himself. Find your freedom by doing first things first. Turn in the New Testament to I John 1:9. Our part is to confess our sin to Him, and thereby we discover He is faithful to Himself and His Word to forgive and cleanse. Commit this verse to your everlasting memory. Once forgiven and cleansed, you are liberated to let this love extend from yourself to others.

One issue in this confession and forgiveness mode bears highlighting. It is no real task for each of us to admit our *missing the mark,* our sin. Binding, cheating, adultery, lying, etc. are easily identified. However, our God has designed us so that if we sincerely desire to relate to Him and receive His promises, this relating is inseparably linked to our relationship with others. It is impossible to love others as ourselves if we are still stashing the unforgiveness card up our sleeves. This is so important that it is the very next teaching after Jesus declared our model prayer in Matthew 6.

While God is interested in how severely we've been wronged, His ultimate plan is that we experience cleansing and restoration. We find in the New Covenant that if we have offended others, we must make honest and sincere effort to seek their forgiveness. In addition, if we have been offended, the judgment is God's, not ours. How grossly erroneous it is for those who haughtily say, "I'll never forgive" or "I may forgive, but I'll never forget". Forgiveness is an act of our will which affects our soul and spirit. We must understand that

God is aware of the clutter that remains in our mental computer. We have the mandate to forgive others and hold not one iota of resentment. Understand that this is not done in our own human strength. Here we need to deal with satan, declaring to him we have forgiven *such and such* so that he cannot torture us anymore. We must be willing to bless if our offender calls for a blessing. This will free us up to receive our Lord's blessing, and discover that we can love others, as we love ourselves.

With What Shall I Mend It?

Our plea for help is to our Lord, the Alpha and Omega, the Savior, the Teacher and Comforter. It is easy to imagine that if anyone is encumbered with loads of excess baggage, it would indeed impede his journey. Yes, we can see this is a journey from darkness, defeat, and self-degradation to entering into light, dispelling darkness and negativity. To seek our own solution from human deduction and opinion is the counterfeit usually at our grasp. Free temporal advice is just that, free and with little or no lasting value. Indeed it is not the basis of our soulish and spiritual transformation. Surface opinions cannot penetrate the depth of the soul.

One sure affirmation we stand upon is God's Word, and His Word is His will, particularly in light of the New Covenant. Therefore, to take a path of renewal in the right direction, our aim and focus must be straight to our Creator/Sustainer/Savior. Our transformation is verified by the fact that His "word is a lamp for my feet, and a light for my path." (Ps. 119:105) His illumination is on our feet to keep us sure-footed, and on our path to keep us on the victorious straight and narrow. This is how we demonstrate that we walk our talk. CINO's, Christians In Name Only, cannot hack it when the chips are down.

An added bonus comes to us from depending on the Word. To pursue wholeness that we can count on, we usually need security and encouragement. Isms and philosophies promise to deliver this. The first problem is that they are not of the one, true, all-righteous God and Father of our Lord Jesus Christ. This is known as missing the mark. Secondly, under close examination it will be noted that these isms and self-improvement schemes are all very self-serving. They all shout, "I want peace. I want tranquility, nirvana, or whatever". None seek the wholeness of the one-on-one relationship with our Almighty God who would spread His blessing *through* us, not just *to* us.

Word For Worth

Of prime importance concerning the Word of God is that it and Jesus Christ are one. In the first verses of the Gospel according to John we quickly discover that "In the beginning the Word already existed. He was with God, and he was God". A similar reference is found in I John 1:1. By the Word, this Redeeming Savior ministers himself to His followers because He is the Living Word. He gave of himself totally that we might know that "overwhelming victory is ours, through Christ, who loved us. (Rom. 8:37) He is glorified in our victory by the power of the Word.

Finally, nearing His departure to go to the right hand of the Father, He assured His followers, even you and me, that He would abide with us in the person of the Comforter, the Holy Spirit. This same Spirit is our teacher, strength, and comfort. This kind of loving provision did not arrive to tolerate our dismay and perplexity. That would go against everything God has revealed and that Jesus taught and did. The Holy Spirit is God's Presence with us to reveal, empower, and take us into victory. If we were not worth redeeming, God would have been foolish to pursue us through His Son, foolish to cause Jesus Christ to bare our sins in His body on the cross. We can only conclude that we must be worth it. He sees and knows our value in Christ Jesus.

This is one of the most mind boggling issues in our faith, that our Lord knows all about us, past and present, and yet loves us anyway. We cannot and must not view our lives by our viewpoint, but by His. Our sin and mistakes are not a hindrance to Him. That is why we call Him our Redeemer. Our redemption to God is when He pays the price, satisfies the demand to *buy us back* from satan's grasp. We become redeemed as God's precious reward.

This calls us to admit that we are worth it. God finds us irresistible to love with His agape love. Binding satan from our lives by being redeemed, we must believe in God's decision and love. The call is to abide in His love and trust in those decisions. Then we can accept our worth and find the way to love our neighbor as ourselves! In His eyes they are worth it, too!

Our God, Your God, All Greatness!!

We who are Bible believers and God-believers, or wannabe's, are favored and blessed to have this frame of reference, this identity. To believe in this God means that we affirm that He is the one, true, living God. This is the one who is the same God of all creation, of Abraham, Isaac, and Jacob. It also defines Him as the Father of our Lord and Savior, Jesus Christ, God's only begotten. All of this is to clarify to whom we are referring. There are religions about this planet which proclaim allegiance to their supreme deity, called by other names, often referred to as "god".

Our God is the one who inspired the early writer to inscribe the Ten Commandments from which our key scripture is derived. When we read, "The second is equally important, love your neighbor as yourself", we recall Jesus repeating this to the lawyer who quizzed him. (Mk. 12:29) The "second" he referred to, of course, was the follower to first commandment just previously mentioned. Possibly if we grasp the greatness of our God, it will help us to realize how important we are to Him. This is where the familiar John 3:16 comes alive.

How Do I Love Thee?

I sn't it magnificent that our God is not some sort of cosmic robot or dictator who merely throws the rules of the game at us and leaves us to sink or swim?! We would then only hear from Him when He blows the whistle at every foul. He it is that wants relationship, eternally, and has gone to every necessary effort to bring us to Him. This we understand as incalculable love. Aren't we thankful that we don't worship some god who wants to enslave the whole world and eliminate those who don't go along?!

Knowing what we know about God and Jesus Christ and their agape love, it stands to reason that whole hearted love from us is to be extended to Him. "We love Him because He first loved us." (I John 4:19 KJV) Our first offering of love to Him is from all our "heart". Of course this is not the muscle which pumps blood, but repeatedly signified in the Bible as our eternal "spirit man". Since we learn in His Word that He is spirit, it is reasonable that our spirits join in love and unity. Jesus affirmed this oneness upon the cross when He uttered, "Father, I entrust my spirit into your hands!" (Lu. 23:46) This type of intimate communion comes from repeated and on-going fellowship. This is where the ministering is mutual. Loving Him with all of our heart denotes feasting on His presence. The beautiful part is that we discover that He reciprocates, confirming our oneness and establishing that trust. As a result it becomes increasingly more important to us to confirm and strengthen that relationship. It is true that we want to be close and in unity with those we love. It is no less true with God. Indeed, He is due and worthy of our praises. We respond positively when someone praises us. It ministers to the spirit man. It is no different with our Heavenly Father. Loving God on the spirit level affirms our trust in His design over His creations, and our desire for oneness with Him.

Soul And Mind

Our key verse, then, exhorts us to love our God with all of our soul. The first clarification facing us concerns the definition of soul. Those who familiarly use the terms "soul brother" or "soul food" have their own connotation for using soul in this case. It seems to refer to individuals who share a likeness with others according to values and race. While this is understandable, it deviates from the Biblical inference as it pertains to the life of God's people.

We have established that, as God views His creation, we are a spirit, we have a soul, and we live in a body. This is the only frame of reference that is coherent with the teachings and revelation of God's Word. Since we have established this order and have addressed the spiritual love, we must confront the issue of the soul. The Biblical understanding of the soul is different from the spirit though they seem somewhat similar inasmuch as they are both intangibles. Most persons love consciously on the soul level, and its application to the body. This is because the soul consists of three elements, namely mind, will, and emotions. As we see, the soul includes the mind which is part of the directive in loving our God.

When we are committing love to our God, or anyone else, we must deal with defining love. It is well understood that the term *love* is defined in three terms: phileo, eros, and agape. The first is demonstrated in the experience of friendship. Eros hints of the type demonstrated as the erotic, the emotional and passionate. Agape is the God-type, completely self-sacrificing and totally committed. To have saved this issue to this part of our journey is by design. To love ourselves or others cannot be reduced to mere emotion. Would it make sense to say in John 3:16 that "God got so emotional toward His creation that He gave His only begotten son . . . ?" To limit oneself to emotion is an invitation to disaster. This is because emotions rise and fall with positive or negative experiences. If God did this, could His love really be depended upon? Is it any different with us?

Though we are not abolishing emotion, we see that love needs a sounder definition. For anyone, including

God, to stay with a person who received His love to the end declares that real and lasting love is a decision, and a commitment. This keeps it from being victim of highs and lows. This is how we understand that we dare not put the cart before the horse, not emotion before decision and commitment. This mistake could be defined as merely emotional affection, devoid of real stability. One might consider emotion akin to the icing on the cake, not the primary item itself. Thus, we can see that loving God with all of our soul and mind is a concrete act of the will. Therefore we are extending our grateful will to our magnificent Heavenly Father. To love self is to will this rightness based on the committed, redeeming quality of Him who made us and intends to see us through.

With Gusto

When something stirs our souls positively, we are incapable of holding back our delight. Yet, the honest truth is that we would have to exert opposing energy to curtail that which would have been natural expression. Who could appear stone-faced and calm upon seeing their new baby for the first time? Such subdued response is possible, but not natural. When you accomplish a goal for which you are primarily if not totally responsible, surely this evokes a response inwardly if not outwardly. Our good God who authors our blessings certainly deserves His honor. However, to restrain oneself or exhibit uncalled-for criticism brings dishonor to our Creator/Sustainer and His Word. We can imagine that He desires our joyous reaction. After all, His Word declares us already as overcomers and "overwhelming victory is ours, through Christ, who loved us.' (Rom. 8:37) This should say something to us about declaring *His* truth, *His* perspective. You can't go wrong; only right!

If you have been a person with a somewhat "average" or "normal" family upbringing, it was probably normal for your parents to show you love, provide for you and give you guidance. Hopefully when you had a great event in your life, they were delighted with your accomplishment and bestowed praise for it. This is the ideal pattern, though we know that no parent is perfect. Consequently, when you are blessed with a special, desired gift or other contribution, your positive response is to express delight and great appreciation. The level of our response basically depends on the value and timeliness of the blessing. If it is timely and met a specific need, then we are more grateful, and that expression would normally be hearty. Then, let us measure this against those times when a very critical need was met. We can understand the delight possibly joined with a sense of relief when it arrived. Normally this evokes expressions of joy along with emotional and physical hugs.

For the believer, and anyone else who wants to render objective thought, we worship and are in relationship with the God who is personable because He is person, the primary of the Trinity. He shall not be limited to intellectual analysis, mere mind. He is not the focal object of positivism. So, when we realize what He has done for us, "while we were still sinners" (Rom. 5:8), as we discover how much He loves us, our loving response should be churning inside. The unfettered reaction from us would be emitting great joy.

This brings up a reassessment on our part in order to get the big picture. When this indescribably great God has gone to cosmic lengths to convey His love through Jesus Christ, we are left with no conclusion but to understand that He must have thought that we were worth it! And indeed, He makes no mistakes. Our blessing and hope is in the Lord Jesus Christ who bore the punishment for all of our sins, past, present and future! The hope in I John 1:9 gives us this access: 'If we confess our sins, He is faithful and just to forgive us and to cleanse us from every wrong." Perhaps His desire for us is to cease our complaints and self-degradation. A simple, "Thank you, Lord" will open the door for cleansing, release, and joy.

Receiving this liberation frees us up not only to love and accept ourselves, but extend that love to others. This is not religion. It is the redemptive relationship with our Creator, Sustainer, and Savior!

Getting It Right with God

Perhaps you have been a believer for a while, or at least you assumed you were. You've been around Christians, maybe even involved in regular worship attendance. Yet, there is still a void which leaves you insecure. Be assured you are not alone, as many are in your same shoes.

You need to understand that this void is by God's design. This is so because it can only be filled by Him. Salvation and walking in His love is His creation and on His terms, not ours. I invite you to settle and secure your relationship with Him once and for all. He is not looking for churchines or religiosity, only honesty and genuine desire.

Just pray the following prayer out loud in your privacy, or accompany by someone you trust. You will begin your wholeness with Him throughout eternity:

> *"Oh God, I come to you because I believe it's right, and what you want. I admit that in my life I have offended others and you, and I am sorry. I ask you to forgive me. I accept that Jesus, your Son, is my Savior, who died in my place to pay the penalty for my sins. I pray that Jesus Christ enters my heart. I ask for your love, and that you lead me to love as you do. Thank you, God. Amen."*

Now, walk one day at a time with God and the Lord Jesus Christ. Depend on Him, and grow inwardly by studying His Word, beginning with the book of the Gospel of John.

In Christ's love,
Paul Allen